DOING CHURCH HISTORY

DOING CHURCH HISTORY

A User-friendly Introduction to
Researching the History of Christianity

Gordon L. Heath

CLEMENTS PUBLISHING
Toronto

Published 2008 by
Clements Publishing
213-6021 Yonge Street
Toronto, Ontario
M2M 3W2 Canada
www.clementspublishing.com

Typeset by Make Design Company
Peterborough, Ontario
www.makedesigncompany.com

Unless otherwise indicated, Scripture is taken from the New Revised Standard Version Bible, copyright © 1989, Division of Christian Education of the National Council of the Churches of Christ in the United States of America

Library and Archives Canada Cataloguing in Publication Data

Heath, Gordon L
Doing church history : a user-friendly introduction to researching the history of Christianity / Gordon L. Heath.

Includes bibliographical references.
ISBN 978-1-894667-90-6

1. Church history—Research—Methodology. 2. Christianity—Research—Methodology. 3. Church history—Historiography. I. Title.

BR138.H38 2008   270.072   C2008-902817-1

v 3.0

Contents

Acknowledgments

As any good historian knows, it is hard to identify all the influences on a person. In regards to the writing of this particular book, just how does one identity all the people and events that led to its writing?

I know that I have benefited from interactions with bright students in my classes that have led to many of my convictions being formed or revised accordingly. I also know that Anthony Bermonte, Nikola Caric, Jamie Robertson and Steve Studebaker, my friends and colleagues who took the time to review the manuscript and make helpful comments and corrections, have directly shaped the contents of this book. Thanks for taking the time.

Finally, I also know that the ones who suffered the most during this project have been my wife Virginia and my children Joshua and Natasha. Thanks for your patience and understanding (and now the bedrooms can get painted!).

Introduction

Death, Taxes, and Church History

The age-old adage is that the two things in life that cannot be avoided are death and taxes. In my experience, those attending seminary often feel like adding church history to that list. Many seminary students are simply not convinced of the need for courses on the history of Christianity, dread taking them, and wish they were eliminated from the curriculum. There are a variety of reasons for such feelings, but two that students have communicated to me over the years are (1) a sense that church history is irrelevant to their ministry training, and (2) a lack of knowledge about the discipline itself (most seminary students do not have a history undergraduate degree). This introduction to historical research will not help seminary students with death or taxes (sorry), but it will provide some simple and straightforward instruction on how to do research in their history of Christianity courses. And in an attempt to convince students that such study is not a waste of time, it will also provide some examples as to why the study of Christian history is important.

While anyone looking for a general introduction to the discipline may find this book helpful, it is written specifically for seminary students preparing for Christian ministry. In my seminary experience both as a student and now as a professor, I have found that there is a need for a basic (and relatively short) introduction to church history. There are other books that should be read by those seeking to go deeper into the discipline. For instance, James E. Bradley and Richard A. Muller's *Church History: An Introduction to Research, Reference Works, and Methods* (Grand Rapids: William B. Eerdmans, 1995) is a helpful guide to the discipline. However, this 200+ page book is quite detailed and dense. It is an important read for those seeking to write a masters or a doctoral thesis in history, and for those seeking to become professional historians, but for students who are only going to take two or three church history courses it is too much. David Bebbington's *Patterns in History: A Christian Perspective on Historical Thought* (Leicester: Apollos, 1979) is another valuable work. However, it too is quite long and detailed, and is really for those who want to go quite a bit deeper into the theoretical and theological issues related to the study of history. Most seminary students do not have the time for (or interest in) an in-depth examination of the discipline of history. What is needed, therefore, is a brief but helpful introduction that provides students with a clear, easy-to-read, and non-technical primer for their history of Christianity courses. By mentioning how history relates to local church situations, and by providing some practical ideas as to how leaders can integrate church history into their ministry, this book should also contribute to the integration of classroom skills and ministry.

There are myriad philosophical and methodological issues that this book has either not addressed or just briefly noted, and the dangers of writing such a non-technical primer are many. Those who come with an undergraduate degree in history may feel as though they are back in Intro to History 101. Those who wish to explore deeply the critical philosophical, theoretical and theological questions will be disappointed with the book's superficiality. Finally, those new to the study of history may think that upon the completion of the reading of this book they have mastered the discipline. Nevertheless, despite these possible disappointments and misconceptions, I am convinced that there is a clear need for this brief book.

The first part of this book deals with some basic theoretical issues regarding the study of the church's history. The second part deals with some foundational how-to elements of the study of history. The bibliography at the back provides further reading for those who desire more depth and analysis. Mastering the discipline of history, and in this case Christian history, is a decades long endeavour, although one that is ultimately rewarding to one's life and ministry. Hopefully, for many students this book is the beginning of such a journey.

Gordon L. Heath
2008

1

The Historian as . . .

"The theologian may indulge the pleasing task of describing Religion as she descended from Heaven, arrayed in her native purity. A more melancholy duty is imposed on the historian. He must discover the inevitable mixture of error and corruption which she contracted in a long residence upon earth, among a weak and degenerate race of beings."

— Jaroslav Pelikan

My experience is that most seminary students have a mental picture of what pastors, preachers, counsellors, or youth workers are supposed to do, but no real mental picture of what historians are supposed to do. What is an historian? What does one do and how is it done? These questions should be relatively easy to answer for those who were history majors in their undergraduate degree. However, for those with other majors, these questions may never have been thought of or even cared about. The problem is that if you are in a church history course, your professor expects you to know the answers to these questions. That being the case, I would like to spend a few moments providing you with some ways to see yourselves as historians. There are other ways, but I find the following three personally satisfying. I also think that they provide a helpful picture of what historians do, how they do it, and why they do it.

WHAT THEY DO: THE HISTORIAN AS TIME TRAVELLER

In order to do a good job, historians must have a sense of imagination and a spirit of adventure, for they must transport themselves back in time to a previous world, a foreign culture, and a different language, a world quite unlike their own. (Their time travel machine is their sources such as books, papers, art and artefacts from the past.)

Through movies such as *Back to the Future* we have been given entertaining glimpses of how travelling back in time is more complicated than it seems. The past is quite unlike the present—and what seems obvious to us is not always the case (e.g. In the first *Back to the Future* movie Marty McFly's female rescuer thought that his name was Calvin Klein because that was the name on his underwear). There is ample room for misunderstandings when travelling in the past, and historians must be able to imagine themselves in the period being studied, and try to understand their subjects in that context.

HOW THEY DO IT: THE HISTORIAN AS A LAWYER

History is not a science in the same way other sciences are sciences. The scientific method is to test one's hypothesis and then revise the hypothesis based on observations. The outcome should be repeatable so as to verify results. However, historians have no such luxury, for what they are studying has already occurred, and cannot be repeated. Consequently, historians have to "get at the truth" through some other means. That means is evidence.

Courtroom TV dramas have given us a picture of the job of a prosecuting attorney. The attorney reconstructs the past using evidence. The various items of evidence are used to build an argument that the case (e.g. "Joe killed his neighbour for rent money") is supported by the evidence (e.g. eyewitnesses, blood samples, murder weapon in Joe's pocket, etc.). The murder cannot be repeated, but it can be reconstructed as far as the evidence allows. Of course, the defence lawyer will attempt to show that there are different interpretations for the evidence. What is important to note in this example is how the criteria for getting at the truth is what is most probable—or beyond a reasonable doubt. There is no scientific, objective way to "prove" that Joe did it. But there is a way to reconstruct the past based on evidence to show that it is most likely, or highly probable, that Joe did it. Historians are like prosecuting attorneys in that they can only reconstruct the past using the available evidence, and that their conclusions are based on what is most probable.

WHY THEY DO IT: THE HISTORIAN AS THE CHURCH'S MEMORY

Alzheimer's disease is a debilitating condition that eventually destroys a person's memory—and through this disease we see how a person cannot function without memory. The same applies for an organization; without a memory the organization is dysfunctional at best, and crippled at worst. John Stackhouse Jr.'s words are worth hearing in this regard:

> Historians function as the memory of the church and we know that people who suffer from a lack of memory have terrible problems. So historians help us see what we have done, help us to learn from our mistakes and equip us with a range of options that have already been tried in the past. History doesn't have all the answers just like our memory doesn't have all the answers, but without memory we waste a lot of time.[1]

By helping the church remember its past, church historians contribute to a healthier church. In the same way, church leaders who help their church remember its past contribute to a healthier church.[2]

---

1. "Sketching the Future," *Envision* (Fall 2000), 12.
2. For a provocative discussion of the need to remember and sometimes to forget, see Miroslav Volf, *The End of Memory: Remembering Rightly in a Violent World* (Grand Rapids: Eerdmans, 2006).

CONCLUSION

There are many different ways to conceptualize historians; time traveller, lawyer and memory are just a few that I find helpful. The chapters that follow will expand upon these images. Before concluding, however, there are a few distinctions that need to be made.

CHURCH HISTORIAN VS HISTORIAN OF CHRISTIANITY

Many who study the church's history do not want to be called church historians. They prefer to be called historians of Christianity (or something quite similar). The reasons for such a distinction are varied. Some prefer the latter because it distances them from any confessional commitment. In other words, historians of Christianity need not be Christians, whereas church historians usually fit within some Christian confession. Others prefer the latter designation because the perception is that the title church historian stresses a study of structure and organization, whereas the title historian of Christianity emphasizes a more widespread study of all forms of the religion. Those within this category would also be scholars who desire to study religion in general and find that the title historian of Christianity is better suited to their discipline. One last reason for not wanting to be called church historian is that no one is a "synagogue historian" or "mosque historian," they are historians of Judaism or historians of Islam. So why not drop church historian and be called an historian of Christianity?

CHRONICLER VS HISTORIAN

I would like to make a distinction between a chronicler and an historian. Without being too simplistic, it is fair to say that a chronicler provides a descriptive and chronological account of an event or events, whereas an historian provides a descriptive, analytical and not necessarily a chronological account of an event or events. Historians offer critical evaluation and critique, whereas chroniclers usually provide a description and leave it at that.

This distinction is not to denigrate the role of a chronicler. Chronicler's are needed and serve a role within the broader discipline. However, what your professors will usually expect in your classes is for you to think, research and write like an historian.

A Chronicle	A History
Based on primary sources, but interaction with secondary sources is limited or nonexistent	Based on primary sources, but interaction with other secondary sources
Usually no thesis	A thesis
Descriptive and usually chronological	Descriptive, analytical and not necessarily chronological
No evaluation	Evaluation & Critique

2

Why Bother?

"Human life without knowledge of history is nothing other than a perpetual childhood, nay, a permanent obscurity and darkness."

— Philip Melanchthon

In an interview recorded in the *Chicago Tribune* in 1916 Henry Ford is reported to have said "History is more or less bunk. It's tradition. We don't want tradition. We want to live in the present and the only history that is worth a tinker's damn is the history we make today."[1] Why not agree with Ford and drop the study of the church's history from the curriculum? It seems obvious why we need to study the Bible, but why study the history of Christianity?

Contrary to Ford's claim is the claim of the sixteenth-century German reformer Philip Melanchthon: "human life without knowledge of history is nothing other than a perpetual childhood, nay, a permanent obscurity and darkness?" Why do I side with Melanchthon? There are a number of reasons why we should commit ourselves to learning as much as possible about the church's history. What follows below is a

---

1. Henry Ford in an interview with Charles N. Wheeler, printed in the *Chicago Tribune*, 25 May 1916.

summary of the key biblical, theological and practical reasons for such a study.

I. BIBLICAL INJUNCTIONS

There are specific biblical injunctions that compel us to learn from the past.

Proverbs

The book of Proverbs instructs us to seek after wisdom. The anonymous medieval saying *historia magistra vitae* ("history, teacher of life") expresses well the reality that we can learn how to live by studying the past. A study of the past is, in many ways, a carrying out of the admonitions of Proverbs to seek after wisdom. Through our study of the past we are seeking to become wise about how to live and serve today.

1 Corinthians 10:11

Paul tells us that certain events in the nation of Israel history were written down as warnings for us today. The general principle being, of course, that we need to learn from the mistakes of the past. But how can we learn from the mistakes of the past if we do not study the past?

Hebrews 11:4

In chapter eleven, the author of the book of Hebrews tried to inspire his faltering readers by listing the many greats of the past. This chapter has been coined the "Faith Hall of Fame" for in its verses are brief summaries of the lives of such heroes as Abel, Enoch, Noah, Abraham, Sarah, Moses, Gideon, Samson, David, and Samuel.

The specific verse that I would like to draw your attention to is 11:4. In the final sentence of that verse we read that "by faith" Abel still speaks to us today. The message is clear: Abel is still speaking, and the others like him in this chapter are still speaking. Our job is to listen. This line reminds me of the movie *The Sixth Sense*. In the movie a young boy named Cole had the ability to see and hear dead people. While most people have five senses (touch, taste, hearing, smell, sight), Cole had a sixth sense: the ability to hear and see dead people. This verse in Hebrews indicates that we, like Cole, can exercise a sixth sense.

The author to the Hebrews does not mean that we are to attempt to communicate with the dead, or listen to some mysterious voices. What is meant is that the example of those listed in this chapter can still speak to us today. If we use our Christian sixth sense—and by faith listen—we will hear their voices, and the voices of those who have lived since that time.

One author that expresses well this idea is Will Durant. In his book *The Lessons of History*, written after he (with the help of his wife) completed his eleven-volume history of civilization, Durant states that

> to those of us who study history not merely as a warning reminder of man's follies and crimes, but also as an encouraging remembrance of generative souls, the past ceases to be a depressing chamber of horrors; it becomes a celestial city, a spacious country of the mind, wherein a thousand saints, statesmen, inventors, scientists, poets, artists, musicians, lovers, and philosophers still live and speak, teach and carve and sing.[2]

If you enjoy the study of history you will know what Durant means. When I walk through an archives, I do not just see old faded papers, or dusty records, or tattered publications. When I walk through the aisles of an archives I see in every journal, every sermon, every biography, and every file of personal correspondence the opportunity to hear voices from the past.

---

2. Will and Ariel Durant, *The Lessons of History* (New York: Simon & Schuster, 1968), 102.

Matthew 22:34–40

Jesus stated that the second greatest commandment was to love one's neighbour. George Marsden writes that love for neighbour requires a study of history:

> The basic reason why we who are Christians should teach and learn history is so that we may better understand ourselves and our fellow men in relation to our own culture and to the world. Since the Christian's task is to live in this world and to witness to the love of God as manifested in Christ, it is essential for us to understand ourselves and the world as best we can. Love is the Christian's central obligation, and understanding is an essential ingredient in love. If we are going to love others, it seems evident that we should try our best to understand them.[3]

It may be too much to say that a lack of interest in the past is an indication of a lack of love for others, but it is probably fair to say that it is difficult to grow in love for others without knowing their past.

II. NATURE OF CHRISTIANITY

One historian claims "Christianity is a religion of historians."[4] One reason for such a bold assertion is that the church has a vested interest in a study of its history. Listen to what Herbert Butterfield says about the necessary link between history and the Christian faith:

> All religions must have their founders, teachers and prophets, and it does not matter if some of these are anonymous or if the historian proves that one or other name amongst them was legendary. Traditional Christianity, however, claims to be an historical religion in a more technical sense; for certain historical events are held to be

---

3. George M. Marsden, "A Christian Perspective for the Teaching of History," in *A Christian View of History?* eds. George M. Marsden and Frank Roberts (Grand Rapids: Eerdmans, 1975), 31–32.

4. Marc Bloch, *The Historian's Craft* (New York: Alfred A. Knopf, 1963), 4.

a part of the religion itself—they are considered to have a spiritual content and to represent the divine breaking in upon history. To a mind which accepts this as revelation—as giving an authentic insight into the real nature of things—there can be no doubt that the whole character of religion itself is seriously affected by the fact.[5]

Christianity is not based on an abstract philosophy, but rather, is based on the belief that God has acted in a very real way in the course of human history. As Colin Brown states, "'belief in' is inseparable from the question of 'belief that.'"[6] As the Apostles Creed so clearly declares, Jesus suffered under Pontius Pilate, was crucified, and then rose again three days later. If these events did not occur Christianity is not true. One example of what I mean is when the apostle Paul said in 1 Corinthians 15 that if the resurrection did not occur then the Christian faith is a waste of time. The truth of the Christian faith is intimately tied to events in human history (no event = no Christianity), therefore, the church has a vested interest in historical events.[7]

Christians also believe that God continues to work in human history, for, as Justo Gonzalez states, God's presence on earth remained after the ascension.[8] In some sense, then, the study of the church's history is a study of God at work. God was at work in the years after Jesus ascended (this is recorded for us in the book of Acts), but that involvement in the life of His people through the work of the Spirit did not end at Acts 28; it has continued throughout the 2000 years since the birth

5. Herbert Butterfield, *Christianity and History* (Fontana Books, 1957), 156.

6. Colin Brown, *History and Faith: A Personal Exploration* (Grand Rapids: Zondervan, 1987), 76.

7. I am aware that some claim that a "Jesus of Faith" is all that one needs. My rejection of such a position is based on passages such as 1 Corinthians 15:14–19, 32.

8. Justo Gonzalez, *The Story of Christianity*, Vol. 1 (San Francisco: Harper, 1984), xvi.

of the church. Church history is in many ways a study of Acts 29 and following.

One other aspect related to the nature of Christianity is the role of tradition. Tradition is a bad word for many Protestants, for that is what Martin Luther and other sixteenth-century reformers fought to free the church from.[9] However, for Roman Catholic and Eastern Orthodox Christians (as well as for some Protestants), tradition plays a critical role in the life of the church. In the best sense of the word, tradition connects us in a very concrete way to the teaching of the apostles, protects us from straying from the apostolic message, and guides us as we seek to live as faithful disciples today. But how can one know the traditions of the church without an understanding of the church's history? Without knowledge of the practices, beliefs and wisdom of the past, how can any person or church remain faithful to the apostolic message once for all delivered to the saints? I like the positive appraisal of tradition that Jaroslav Pelikan provides when he writes: "Tradition is living faith of the dead, traditionalism is the dead faith of the living. And, I suppose I should add, it is traditionalism that gives tradition such a bad name."[10]

III. PRACTICAL REASONS

Besides the more lofty biblical and theological reasons, there are a number of practical reasons why Christians can and should study church history.

---

9. For a helpful recent discussion of the necessary role of tradition among evangelical Protestants, see D.H. Williams, *Retrieving the Tradition & Renewing Evangelicalism: A Primer for Suspicious Protestants* (Grand Rapids: Eerdmans, 1999) and D.H. Williams, *Evangelicals and Tradition: The Formative Influence of the Early Church* (Grand Rapids: Baker, 2005).

10. Jaroslav Pelikan, *The Vindication of Tradition* (Yale University Press, 1984), 64.

The Common Human Condition

Machiavelli declared "Whoever wishes to foresee the future must consult the past; for human events ever resemble those of preceding times. This arises from the fact that they are produced by men who ever have been, and ever shall be, animated by the same passions, and thus they necessarily have the same results." We today are basically the same as our forbearers (motivated by greed, love, ambition, lust, idealism, glory, faith, etc.), and therefore we have much in common and much to learn from those who have come before us.

Learn from the Past

George Santayana has stated "Those who cannot learn from history are doomed to repeat it." Imagine if one had to learn over and over again that a hot stove element should not be touched! Studying and remembering what does and does not work is a reason to study the past.

Provides Perspective

After 9/11, I had a student ask me "how could God have allowed this to happen?" Anyone with even a modicum of historical knowledge would have known that far greater tragedies have happened in human history. Without knowledge of the horrors of the plague, Stalin's Gulags, the Holocaust or other mind-boggling tragedies, we can lose perspective and think that our own generation's injustices are the greatest crimes. We can also lose our faith if we think that God only allows good things to happen. A quick reading of history inoculates us against being surprised when confronted with heinous evil and appalling injustice.

Helps Us to Escape the Pressing Voices of the Present

In his defence of academic studies during the Second World War, C. S. Lewis stated that a study of the past was necessary in order to hear properly and gain some perspective on the many and varied voices that demanded attention: "A man who has lived in many places is not likely to be deceived by the local errors of his native village: the scholar has lived in many times and is therefore in some degree immune from the

great cataract of nonsense that pours from the press and the micro-
phone of his own age."[11] While there is no guarantee, knowledge of
the past should allow us to see things a bit more clearly and to ignore
some of the more pressing and sensational messages that bombard us
everyday.[12]

Reminded of the Reality of Life and Death

Every time you see the two dates beside a person's name you are
reminded of the reality of life and death. Everyone, even the most
famous, has only a brief time on earth, and every history text blares this
to its readers. Thoughtful readers will be challenged to think about the
use of their own lives, for, as one of my students has noted, everything
you did, thought and said in life will be represented by the dash on your
tombstone between the two dates.

Understand the Church's Roots (like a family tree)

Ortega y Gasset has said "each generation stands on the shoulders
of its predecessors like acrobats in a vast human pyramid. Thus to tell
the story of those whose heirs we are is to write a long preface to our
own life stories."[13] Knowing the church's history is like knowing your
family tree. And just like there is an intangible sense of identity when
one's family tree is known, there is a sense of belonging when you know
where your church, denomination and faith have come from over the
past 2000 years.

Better Understand Theology

What do you say to a Jehovah's Witness who comes to your door
and claims that Jesus was the first created being? How do you begin

---

11. C.S. Lewis, "Learning in War-time," in *The Weight of Glory and
Other Addresses* (Grand Rapids: Eerdmans, 1965), 50–51.

12. Remember that some of the first and most ardent supporters of
Nazism were university professors (historians included) and university students.

13. As quoted in Gonzalez, *The Story of Christianity*, Vol. 1, xiii.

to understand the differences between Roman Catholicism and Protestantism? A study of the church's history will help you place modern day claims such as Jesus being a created being in the larger context of the church's treatment of fourth-century Arianism (a movement that claimed that Jesus was the first created being). How did the church deal with it then, and how does that inform our modern-day response to similar claims? Knowledge of the Reformation will certainly assist in understanding why there are fundamental differences and significant similarities between Catholics and Protestants. Over and over again a study of the church's history will help you understand contemporary theological dilemmas, which is indispensable for working with people from diverse Christian backgrounds.

Clarifies the Nature of Discipleship and Leadership

No "greats" or saints of the past ever took or had an easy road. In fact, even a cursory reading of the history of the church indicates that true discipleship costs everything, and meaningful leadership is painful. Perpetua's imprisonment and martyrdom, Athanasius' repeated exiles, Francis of Assisi's poverty, Luther's trials, Wilberforce's defeated motions, and Mother Theresa's sacrifices all speak powerfully to the true nature of discipleship and leadership. Life in the Kingdom of God is not about wealth, power or prestige, it is about poverty, self-control, self-denial and obedience to Christ. If you want to make a difference with your life, read the lives of the "greats" to be reminded of what it takes to be a disciple and leader.

Helps in Leadership Issues

Having experimented with the way in which communion was served I was quickly (and harshly) told by a parishioner that communion was the "one immutable" thing in the church—and should never be changed. If that person had known the history of the church he would have never said that to me (a minister in training), for communion has been—and is—celebrated in numerous ways. Certainly knowledge of the past helps church leaders know their particular tradition and work within it. However, rather than simply lock a church in the past, a study of the church's history also frees it to try new things in new ways. Why? A study of the past shows that there have been numerous ways in which things have been done, and there have been countless innovative methods of reaching cultures for Christ.

Encourages Humility

It only takes a few minutes of reading about the Inquisition or the Wars of Religion in the sixteenth and seventeenth centuries to see how many Christians have been quite wrong in their understanding of what God expects. If others could be so wrong, we should in humility consider how we may also be wrong.

Rich Devotional & Liturgical Material

The wealth of resources in the past cannot be overestimated. Rich devotional writings, poems, prayers, liturgies, and the like are available for us to draw upon today. We ignore these resources at our peril. Hear what one historian says about these resources:

> But there have been over seventy generations of Christians since the time of the apostles. Just think of the dragon's hoard of theological, devotional and intellectual treasure that waits you as you explore those seventy generations. Every generation is equidistant from the Holy Spirit. Ours is not privileged in this respect. So when you study church history, you would be wise to bring a pick and shovel and chest to carry away treasure.[14]

Helps in Apologetics

How does one begin to address hostile claims about the church's past when one does not even know the past? To be ignorant of the church's history is to place yourself in the unenviable position of having to defend or explain the past without even knowing much or anything about it.

---

14. D. Bruce Hindmarsh, "On Not Forgetting the Story of the Church," *Crux* 40 (December 2004): 3.

Influence of Christianity in the West

Much of the Western world has been shaped by Christianity (e.g. politics, morality, philosophy), and to neglect the history of the church is to neglect a significant portion of history in general. Such neglect would also lead to an impoverished understanding of one's own culture.

Provides Inspiration

The sixteenth-century Swiss reformer Ulrich Zwingli declared "To know the limbs and leaps of history is hardly worth a cent . . . The only thing which counts is that you become more certain of your God as you contemplate the past, and that you show more courage in the face of present needs!"[15] Everyone needs a hero, and a study of the church's heritage can provide just that. A study of the church's history can also make us more confident in our God as we face the trials and tribulations of discipleship and leadership.

---

15. Gonzalez, *The Story of Christianity*, Vol. 1, xiii.

3

A Brief History of Church History[1]

"All great human causes turn on theories of history."

— Charles A. Beard

While all historians share a common interest in the past, all historians are not alike. Some historians are military historians, interested in battles fought and weapons used. Others are political historians, interested in politics and the decisions of governments. Still others are social historians, focused on the everyday events and concerns of the common person. Historians can also be identified by their concerns, such as feminist historians, or methodologies, such as Marxist historians. Church historians are just one type of historian, and it is to the history of such historians that we now turn.[2]

---

1.   Much of this material is taken from Mark T. Gilderhus, *History and Historians: A Historiographical Introduction* (Prentice Hall, 2000), ch.2; Ernst Breisach, *Historiography: Ancient, Medieval, and Modern 2nd ed.* (University of Chicago Press, 1994), 77-82. For a helpful survey of significant Christian historians, see Michael Bauman & Martin L Klauber, eds., *Historians of the Christian Tradition: Their Methodology and Influence on Western Thought* (Nashville: Broadman and Holman Publishers, 1995).

2.   For a summary of some of the major types of historians or methodologies, see the chart at the end of this chapter.

Ancient religious myths, legends and fables were meant to inspire, rather than inform (therefore, events could remain timeless). Some accounts spoke of a direct relationship between humans and the gods, and these gods and/or goddesses often had human characteristics, and achieved their purposes through their control of "lesser" beings. In Greek mythology they were often in competition with one another, often cruel, and seen to be the cause of disasters. The Greek idea of "hubris" (self-destructive pride) meant that the gods were required to strike down anyone who overreached his/her place in life (or even nations such as Persia).

The Jews of ancient history had quite a different view of history. Out of all the ancients, history was most important for the Jews. The Jews believed that their God had established a special relationship with them. He had chosen them as His special people to fulfill certain obligations. The Jews saw the hand of God in human affairs; God rewarded and blessed the good, and punished the evil. As you know, the Jews recorded their history in the Old Testament. Their writing of history, however, was not *per se* a rational inquiry into the past. Rather, it was written to record the way in which God had acted in their history. The exodus, the great redemption event of the Old Testament, was a historical deliverance at the hand of God. It was also a history that was, at times, quite honest. For example, the history of the kings reveals warts and all (e.g., David's adultery and murder).

The pagan and early Christian inhabitants of the Roman Empire lived in two radically different mental worlds. When it came to history, the Romans identified the past, present and future with the Roman State. Early Christians, on the other hand, were not that concerned with such things. They stressed the Jewish view that God had acted in history, and was not like the Greek or Roman gods who acted arbitrarily or capriciously. On the contrary, God guided and directed all events towards the fulfillment of his plans. Furthermore, Christian's believed that the Incarnation made a Roman or Greek view of history impossible (e.g. not cyclical, or left to Fate or Fortune). The Incarnation was considered to be central to the course of all human history; all of human history was considered to be moving towards Christ's return to earth. Historical knowledge was very important for early Christians, for their faith was built on the conviction that certain events had actually occurred (e.g. Incarnation, Passion, resurrection), and as the faith spread throughout the empire there was a need to affirm the veracity of the apostolic claims.

The conversion of Constantine in the early fourth century led to the writing of the first history of the church (if you do not count Luke's Acts): Eusebius of Caesaria's *Ecclesiastical History*. It had a polemical edge to it, for he was certainly writing a history to validate the new faith in the eyes of pagans. It was a Bishop from North Africa, however, who in the early fifth century formulated the most influential Christian interpretation of history. St. Augustine's *City of God* influenced the next 1,000 years of Christian history writing.

Some of the characteristics of the Christian view of history throughout the medieval period were:

- Jesus was the central event of all human history (in many accounts, a "universal" history was presented, beginning with creation, through the Old Testament and New Testament, up to what God had been doing in the present)

- Human history was not cyclical, but rather, moving in a linear way towards a specific end

- God was providentially guiding events towards his purposes

A key word to note here is teleology. "Teleology involves uncovering great developmental patterns in history that show either progress or decline"[3] towards a specific end or telos. For Christian historians,

---

3. Norman J. Wilson, *History in Crisis: Recent Directions in Historiography* (Prentice Hall, 1999), 7. On page 8 he writes: "Teleology frequently results in a history of the winners without adequate consideration of other outcomes that might have occurred . . . Teleology cannot be avoided, but it can be curtailed to tolerable levels by resisting the temptation to find a goal toward which history is supposedly moving. One way to avoid overly teleological history is to consider how things could have happened differently."

history moved teleologically according to design toward a foreordained conclusion. Most histories in the medieval period focused on sacred history, rather than the secular, with the purpose of outlining God's work in the world.

Certain Renaissance historians began to move away from this God-centered view of history, but the Reformation historians did not. Whether Protestant or Roman Catholic, church leaders who invoked history were convinced that God acted in human history, and that God was acting on their side.

Enlightenment historians continued the Renaissance trend of a secular history. Three of the foremost historians of the Enlightenment, Voltaire, Hume and Gibbon, depreciated the role of religion, and saw it as an impediment to human progress. Regarding these three, one historian writes: "It is one of the glories of the eighteenth century that it produced within a generation three of the world's greatest historians: Voltaire, Hume and Gibbon, all grounded in philosophy, seeking to reinterpret history in non-theological terms . . . All three of these historians agreed in exposing superstition, rejecting supernatural explanations, and identifying progress with the development of knowledge, manners, and arts."[4] By the late nineteenth century the scientific study of history had led to significant advances in the professionalization of the discipline of history, but had also led to many writing the church's history apart from any supernatural explanations or teleology.

There are still those today who write the history of the church as "His-story," a history of God's providential workings among his people and for his plans. There are other histories of the church that avoid providential language, and emphasize what can be seen and known by a study of visible evidence. Some of the questions surrounding these two ways of writing the history of Christianity are dealt with in the following chapters.

---

4. Will and Ariel Durant, *The Age of Voltaire*, Vol. 9 (Simon and Schuster, 1965), 156.

TYPES OF HISTORY

Methodology	Focus	Comments
Political History	Key events, people or battles. Concerned with providing a grand explanation for the "important" things	The more traditional type of history that focuses on political events and people, or on important military battles. Research for this type of work was usually based on official documents such a minutes, hansard, or papers from key leaders.
Marxist History	Economic or material factors that motivated behaviour. Concerned with the ongoing war between the proletariat and the bourgeoisie.	A twentieth-century phenomenon. Research often based on same sources as political histories, but looks behind the stated reasons to discover the material motives for actions.
Social History	The "little" or powerless person, or everyday life. Concerned with looking at voices or groups that have been ignored in the more traditional forms of historical research. Oftentimes referred to as "history from below."	A post-Second World War phenomenon. Research for this type of history will try to find different voices by (a) trying to hear the voices of the powerless in official documents, or (b) trying to discover new untapped sources that provide a voice for the powerless or exploited. This type of approach is popular among post-modern and post-colonial historians who are trying to hear from the oppressed, not the hegemonic powers.
Feminist History	The lives of women. A significant overlap with social history, in that the voices of the marginalized (in this case women) are the focus of attention.	A post-Second World War phenomenon. Much like social history, this type of history will try to find female voices by (a) trying to hear their voices in official documents, or (b) trying to discover new untapped sources that provide a women's perspective.

Intellectual History	The history of ideas. Concerned with the history of ideas, and the people that have written and propagated them	Research for this type of work usually concentrates on the published writings of key intellectuals or authors and their ideas that have helped to shape the world.
Historical Theology	Theology, but with a particular emphasis on the historical context in which theological statements were formulated. Similar to intellectual history in that both are concerned with ideas, but ideas in a particular historical context.	Like intellectual history, research for this type of work usually concentrates on the published writings of key theologians or authors and their ideas that have helped to shape the world.
Church History	The Christian church. Concerned with the historical development of the church, and (in some cases) a providential explanation of events.	The more traditional type of church history focused on official documents. More recently historians concerned with the history of Christianity have also sought to look at sources not usually looked at (e.g. voices of women, children, heretics, newspapers). Many have also moved away from providential explanations.

4

What about God as a Cause?

"On 2 July 1098, when the siege by the Turks had lasted
for three weeks and four days, we went out with all our
equipment of war, seeking the city gates. After firmly ordering
our battle-lines, of both foot and horse, we boldly sought the
place where their valour and bravery were the greatest. The
Holy Lance was with us, and from the very first engagement
of the battle we forced the enemy to flee . . . and the grace
and mercy of God came to our aid, so that we, who were
very few compared with them, still managed, for the right
hand of God fought with us, to drive them together and to
force them to flee, leaving their camp and all its contents.
Bohemund of Antioch received the citadel and a thousand
Muslim men, and so our Lord Jesus Christ transferred the
whole city of Antioch to the Roman religion and faith."

— Radulph of Caen

On the one hand there is no difference between doing Christian history and history. In both cases, evidence needs to be considered, arguments formed and probabilities considered. Whether it is Christian hockey or hockey, Christian carpentry or carpentry, Christian auto mechanics or auto mechanics, the rules are the same. On the other hand, there are convictions that distinguish Christian views of history from other views of history. One conviction that has the most direct (and controversial) relationship with historical research is that of providence.

37

I. WHAT ABOUT CAUSES?

In one of my classes two students wrote on what caused the Protestant Reformation. One student wrote that God providentially decided to renew his church, and so God caused it. To support the claim the student quoted a variety of biblical texts that showed that God wanted a pure church. Another student wrote a paper that listed the many social, political, cultural, theological and personal reasons why the Reformation occurred when it did. To support this claim various examples were provided of what seemed to be precursors to the Reformation (e.g. development of the printing press, anti-clerical sentiment in Germany, rising German nationalism). Which student was right? Could both be right?

If any chapter of this book produces discussion or controversy it will be this one, for it deals with a central Christian conviction and addresses a topic over which even historians differ. As noted in the previous chapter, for centuries Christian historians believed in God's providence *and* wrote their histories with a sense that providence could be discerned and the hand of God identified. Due to a variety of factors, the history of the church is increasingly written without this "bird's eye view" of its past. More often the events of the church's past are explained by identifying the human causes "on the ground" (e.g. key people, movements, ideas, battles). What is the right approach? How should God-as-a-cause be written into church histories? The following is a brief summary of how I reconcile my Christian convictions regarding providence with those of the academy that emphasize analysis and evidence. Of course, you would be wise to inquire about your own professor's views and expectations before doing your assignments.

Please note that this question is not just an academic one, it is a pastoral one as well. Christian leaders are often called upon to discern a divine interpretation of events and say what God did, or did not, do, and why events occurred. For instance, at a funeral people want to know why the car's brakes did not work, or why the fire alarms were not heard. What did God cause? Can past events be explained by simply pointing to causes "on the ground" (e.g. poor maintenance) or by a "bird's eye view" (e.g. God wanted to teach you something by allowing the death)? What is the meaning behind the tragedy? In other words, both Christian historians and church leaders need to know how to write and speak about providence. In both cases, the core issues are the same.

II. KNOWING THE MIND OF GOD?

As noted above, for centuries Christian historians wrote as though they could discern God's hand in events. For instance:

- The conversion of Emperor Constantine in 312 C.E. was hailed as the working of God
- Divine providence was proclaimed to be the reason for the crusader's victories over the Muslims in the First Crusade
- The defeat of the Roman Catholic Spanish Armada in 1588 was explained by Protestants in England as the direct intervention of God. It was said by Protestants that "God breathed and they were scattered."

These examples are but the tip of the iceberg of how historians have claimed to know what certain events meant. But do we really know that God caused these events, and why he caused them? Do we really know the providential meaning of these events? Rather than go into a complex theological and philosophical discussion of God's sovereignty and human free will, et al., the following is a summary of what I consider to be the critical issues and way forward in this discussion. Of course, for those who would like to grapple further with this issue, the bibliography at the end of this book provides suggested readings.

III. LONGING FOR MEANING

It must be admitted that the longing for meaning is powerful. To memorize the dates and events of the past without ascribing any grand meaning to them can be depressing. For some, there is no other choice; looking for meaning is naïve and ultimately futile. For others who believe in some point to history there is a choice, and a need. One extreme contemporary example would be the Hal Lindsey phenomenon of identifying almost every major world event (especially Middle Eastern events) as having some profound meaning and place in God's great plan of salvation and history. Less extreme examples also abound, for the Christian conviction that God has a plan, and the human need to have meaning, coalesce in Christian attempts to make sense of what has happened. The "response to the catastrophes of our secular age and the search for an alternative view of human nature and human history"[1] has made the quest for meaning all the more pressing, for the old answers seem empty and new ones need to be found. We must be aware of these pressures, and be careful not to superimpose supernatural meaning on events that we have no evidence for, despite our strong feelings that our explanation makes sense.

IV. PROVIDENCE

Regardless of how particular historians write their church history, a core Christian conviction is that God is at work in history, and that the coming of Jesus Christ is at the heart of that work. As James M. Boice notes:

> The secular historian might judge that the coming of Jesus was
> a pivotal event because of his obvious influence on later history.
> But the Christian conviction, symbolized by the division of time,
> goes beyond that recognition. As Cullmann says, 'The modern

---

1. C.T. McIntire, "Introduction" in *God, History, and Historians: An Anthology of Modern Christian Views of History*, ed. C.T. McIntire (New York: Oxford University Press, 1977), 6.

historian may when pressed find a historically confirmed meaning in the fact that the appearance of Jesus of Nazareth is regarded as a decisive turning point in history. But the *theological* affirmation which lies at the basis of the Christian chronology goes far beyond the confirmation that Christianity brought with it weighty historical changes. It asserts rather that from this mid-point all history is to be understood and judged.' Christianity affirms that apart from Christ there is no way of determining what history as a whole is all about, nor can we legitimately weigh historical events so that one may be pronounced better or more significant than another. With Christ, however, both those essentials for a true historical outlook are provided.[2]

Along with the conviction that Jesus is at the center of all human history is the belief that God still works in history, is in control of history, and is moving it towards its ultimate consummation (when Christ returns). One last conviction needs to be added: God works in, upon and through his people. As Martin Luther wrote: "God alone is in this business [reforming of the church]; we are seized so that I see we are acted upon rather than act."[3] It seems to me that this summary is a fairly simplistic, but biblical, précis of the traditional meaning of providence. Of course, the question still remains, how do we bring this conviction to bear in our historical research?

V. WHO SAID WE COULD KNOW?

Where does the doctrine of providence indicate that we could know what God is up to? Better yet, what biblical passages indicate that we can know the mind and plans of God so clearly that we can say with assurance that we know what caused this or that, and why? Yes, prophets such as Isaiah knew why God's people were being invaded

---

2. James Montgomery Boice, *God and History* (Downers Grove: Inter-Varsity Press, 1981), 46.

3. As quoted in John M. Headley, *Luther's View of Church History* (New Haven: Yale University Press, 1963), 1.

from the north. But they were prophets, unique among the people (and even they did not know why everything happened). For the rest of us, passages such as Romans 11:33–36 are more relevant, for they indicate our inability to know what God is up to. To claim that we cannot know why God caused (or allowed) certain events does not necessarily undermine the Christian doctrine of providence, it just says that there are some things for which we need faith. C. S. Lewis was convinced that historians could not claim to interpret providence (he called historians who made such claims historicists). He wrote that the conditions for such knowledge were just not possible:

> If, by one miracle, the total context of time were spread out before me, and if, by another, I were able to hold all that infinity of events in my mind and if, by a third, God were pleased to comment on it so that I could understand it, then, to be sure, I could do what the Historicist says he is doing. I could read the meaning, discern the pattern. Yes; and if the sky fell we should all catch larks.[4]

History has a purpose, but the reason(s) and ultimate outcome(s) for historical events remain a mystery. What is only required is faith to believe that God is at work, in control, and is moving history towards its final consummation.

In this regard I find Martin Luther helpful. Luther stated that history was a mask behind which God works. God is certainly at work in the world. He is not only at work through Christ and the Word, but also in created orders and offices. One's home, school, work, and community comprise these created orders, and it is these orders that are considered to be masks of God. Behind and through these masks of creation God is at work, and it is only through faith that a Christian may see these masks (or events) as coming from God. These masks, however, do not reveal all that there is to know about God, for like the masks of actors on a stage they not only reveal but also conceal. History, therefore, has

---

4. C. S. Lewis, "Historicism," in *God, History and Historians*, ed. C. T. McIntire (New York: Oxford University Press, 1977), 229.

a purpose, but the reason(s) and ultimate outcomes for such events remain a mystery. Historical events may reveal something of God and His purposes, but these same revelatory events also conceal the plans and purposes of God. What is only required is faith; faith to believe that God is at work, and faith to believe that all is under His control.

VI. NOT A GREAT TRACK RECORD

A very practical reason for questioning claims of knowing why God did this or that is that so many times historians have contradicted themselves or have been just plain wrong. While some Christians today may praise the day Constantine was converted, many others now see it as the beginning of the decline of the early church's focus and purity, and the beginning of its unholy alliance with the state. Although there are some, no doubt, who still attribute the crusader's initial successes to the "hand of God," the slaughters, rapes, pillaging, and desecrations that were part of the crusades lead most Christians to reject claims that their successes were the result of God's miraculous interventions. Certainly the Protestants saw the defeat of the Spanish Armada as God's intervention, but what of the Catholic interpretation? In all of these cases, trends (a move from persecution to political power), theology (pilgrimages and holy war), political loyalties (anti-Spanish English nationalism), or religious affiliation (Catholic or Protestant) influenced how Christians interpreted the historical events unfolding around them. Even if we could step outside of our culture long enough to be able to see things more clearly, there is no reason to think that we could know why God did what he did, or know what he is doing in the world.

VII. A SOLUTION?

For the above-mentioned reasons, I am reticent to claim that God caused this or that to happen, or to claim that I know why God allowed something to occur. However, this does not contradict my earlier claim that church history is a study of Acts 29 and following, and a story of God's working in the life of his people.

In fact, the solution that I propose is very much modelled on the dynamics seen in the book of Acts: God was at work in his people, and his people were very much at work. The Spirit's work in the book of Acts was through the decisions and actions of the earliest Christians, and their activities certainly had a part to play in how the church's earliest decades unfolded. The same is true today. I like how Mark Noll states this divine-human interplay in his recent book on the birth of evangelicalism. He writes:

> However one regards the work of the Holy Spirit in the evangelical movement, the Spirit was certainly putting to use channels of influence from the domains of ordinary history. Those channels were many, but why they worked to different effects in different regions and on different individuals only the closest attention to sources and the most multidimensional explanations can say.[5]

What our historical research focuses on are the "channels of influence from the domains of ordinary history." Unless you are a prophet like Isaiah or Jeremiah receiving revelations directly from the Lord informing you of God's sovereign plan and purposes, you do not know the providential perspective. But what we can all do is strive to study how human decisions have impacted the church's course, for there are still many lessons to be learned through a study of the church's history.

Does this approach deprive us of the consolations of the doctrine of providence? Some may say yes, for there is hope to be found in knowing what God's plans are for the church and nation. But I say not at all. Christians do not need to know the inner counsels of the Trinity in order to receive comfort from knowing that God is at work in, and in control of, history. Besides, the Christian's hope lies in the ultimate

---

5. Mark Noll, *The Rise of Evangelicalism: The Age of Edwards, Whitefield and the Wesleys* (IVP, 2003), 154.

return and triumph of Christ, not in knowing the answers to all the whys of history.[6]

---

6. As a counterpoint to my comments here is the position of David Bebbington. Bebbington agrees that that there have been serious mistakes made by those who have claimed to know what God was up to. However, he also states that there is still a need for Christian historians to speak of providence (but do it wisely). He writes "The Christian historian can discern God at work in the past without necessarily writing of him there. This approach is nothing other than the Christian attitude to living carried over into historical work. In ordinary life, believers do not always make Christian claims explicit at all times. They do so when it is appropriate, whether within the Christian community or in apologetics and evangelism. Similarly, the Christian historian is not obliged to tell the whole truth as he sees it in every piece of historical writing. He can write of providence or not according to his judgment of the composition of his audience." He goes on to write about how the church needs, at times, Christian historians to encourage the church by reminding it of God's providence. See Bebbington, *Patterns in History*, 187. The difficulty, of course (and as Bebbington knows), is being able to discern God's providence.

5

What Caused It?

*"The older I get the more I'm convinced that it's
the purpose of politicians and journalists to say
the world is very simple, whereas it's the purpose of
historians to say, 'No! It's very complicated.'"*

— David Cannadine

One of the most common questions historians have to answer is why something occurred. However, if we need to avoid making statements about God causing events, what can we say about other causes? While at first glance it may appear to be quite easy to understand why something occurred, further analysis usually makes it apparent that things are not always so clear. Some of the reasons for such ambiguity are:

- We were not there to see the events (even if we were there we see only from our own perspective).
- We are limited in our analysis by the sources available for study.
- The sources never provide all the information we need.
- Our sources may give us details of what happened, but they rarely provide such intangibles as emotions and motives (often the most important factors in why something occurred!)

- Actions are very difficult to interpret for actions can arise out of many different motives. In fact, the exact same actions in two different people could be done for two very different reasons.
- The distinction between a cause of an event and something that facilitated the event is often blurred (and even making this distinction is often hard to do).
- A number of events may occur concurrently, but be completely unrelated.

Perhaps a few examples of the difficulties of making causal connections will suffice. First, I have read (and heard from the pulpit) that the Roman Empire collapsed in the fifth century due to its immorality. In other words, the cause of the empire's woes was the deleterious effect of immorality on the citizenry of Rome. The problem with such a view is that we could ask the question why did the effects of the immorality happen in the fifth century? Why not the second, third or fourth (when there was just as much sin)? Also, the eastern part of the empire with its capital city of Constantinople continued for a thousand years after the fall of the western empire. Why did the effects of the sins of Rome stop at the border and not go further east? And why did other equally sinful empires not fall? The cause of the collapse of the western empire must be more complex than just sin. Second, what caused the First World War? Was it a rigid alliance system? A military build up? German nationalism? All of these things existed before the early twentieth century, so why did the war happen in 1914, and not in 1887, or 1892, or 1911, or 1919 (or some other date)?

Like many issues related to historical studies, this is not just an ivory tower discussion. The question of cause will be one that you face in Christian leadership and ministry. Why is the church not growing (or why is it growing)? Why did the pastor get fired? Why did the church split? Who is to blame for the marriage breakdown? Why did the child run away? These are all historical questions related to cause.

Difficulties do not mean that we should avoid dealing with causes, they simply mean that we must be ever-so-careful about making causal connections. The following questions should be kept in mind when attempting to identify why something occurred:

- What direct connection is there between the event and what you have identified as a cause? What evidence do you have to support this connection?

- If motives are stated, what are they? Can you believe them? What motives may not be stated (and why)? Remember that people usually do something for more than one motive, and often do things for reasons that they do not know.

- What other factors may explain the event in question?

- Are there a variety of accounts as to why something occurred (e.g. different eyewitness accounts)? If so, how can the views be reconciled?

- What key people were involved? What key issues were factors? What key ideas played a role in shaping opinions?

- What was a direct cause and what more indirectly facilitated the events? (For instance, was the printing press a cause of the Reformation, or did the printing press facilitate the growth and success of the Reformation?)

- What critical theories may help you identify causes? And what critical theories may distract from identifying real causes?

Paying attention to these questions should help you as you attempt to get at the roots of why something occurred. Perhaps the most basic bit of advice to remember is that almost every event has more than one cause, for life is complicated and your research should reflect that.

6

What About Objectivity?

"Who does not know history's first law to be that an author must not dare to tell anything but the truth? And its second that he must make bold to tell the whole story?"

— Cicero

I. A MATTER OF PROBABILITY

The movie *12 Angry Men* (1957, 1997) portrays a jury deliberating over the evidence of a murder trial. The jury's struggles are a vivid example of the difficulty of trying to reconstruct the past. The evidence can often be interpreted more than one way, and the personalities and motives of the interpreters certainly play a part in the interpretive process. These are the struggles that every historian faces.

The study of history uses a different type of "proof" than other disciplines/sciences. For example, chemists use the scientific method for their experiments, and they observe their test results in real time. Historians cannot do that, for what they are studying has already happened, and cannot be repeated. As a result, they use a different type of proof that by its very nature is less objective than other sciences.[1]

---

1. Over the past few decades the ability of any scientists to be purely objective has been questioned.

All this is to say pure objectivity is not possible for historians. Unlike some sciences, historians deal with possibilities and probabilities. The question for historians is whether or not something can be known with a degree of confidence.

II. PREVIOUS OPTIMISM

There have been many great historians who were quite confident that they could know the truth about the past. One of the most famous nineteenth-century historians was Leopold von Ranke (1795–1886). He played an instrumental role in the establishment of history as a separate discipline. For Ranke, the discipline of history was concerned with the collection of facts and the gaining of knowledge of what actually happened. Confidence to show "what actually happened" was a mark of those who followed in his footsteps.

III. CONTEMPORARY SCEPTICISM

For many today such Rankean optimism seems too good to be true or naïvely hopefully. The reasons for such a shift in confidence are complex, but the influence of deconstructionism and postmodernism on the discipline has led to a great deal of scepticism surrounding any claim of knowing something (or even anything) about the past.

This is not the place for a full-scale treatment of either movement. Suffice it to say that both are, in the most basic sense, systems that distrust what appears to be the "obvious" written word, and systems that question motives and intentions. However, the drawback of some radical proponents is that the intention of the author becomes at best, a secondary concern, or at worst, an irrelevant (or unknowable) matter. Frederick Crews in the *Postmodern Pooh* provides a humorous but scathing critique of many contemporary literary theories that, when applied to the Winnie the Pooh stories, reveal a children's story full of same sex marriage (piglet moves in with Pooh), misogyny (Kanga's oppressed state at home), abuse (Piglet's behavior is obviously a sign of an abusive past) and even imperialism (Pooh's attempts to steal honey from the bees).[2] I have no desire to go into the wars over postmodernism in my discipline, other than to point out that our ability to know the past through documents with any degree of certainty is definitely challenged by such assumptions and methodology.

IV. IMPLICATIONS OF RADICAL SCEPTICISM

The claim that truth, including truth about the past, is perspectival, in the eye-of-the-reader, or simply unattainable is problematic for a few reasons.

Historical Studies in General, and Holocaust Denial in Particular

Richard Evans argues in his book *In Defence of History* that extreme relativism leaves the door "wide open" to holocaust deniers.[3] How can anyone say that holocaust deniers are wrong when their view must be put on par with the traditional view (with no way of determining which is the right view)? For anyone concerned with refuting a particular view of the past, postmodernism's emphasis on multiple narratives or truth being perspectival is problematic. The larger question is, of course, if tens of thousands of living eyewitnesses of the Holocaust cannot be trusted, how can any study of the past be trusted?[4] Historical research, therefore, must be a waste of time.

The Christian Faith

If there is no way of having a degree of confidence about what happened in the past, then we as Christians are in trouble. This is not necessarily Evans' concern, but it should be ours. Christians believe that God has not just intervened in human history, but has also entered into human history (the Incarnation). But if we cannot speak with a

---

2. Frederick Crews, *Postmodern Pooh* (New York: North Point Press, 2001).

3. Richard Evans, *In Defence of History* (London: Granta Books, 1997), 238–243.

4. Richard Evans, *Lying About Hitler: History, Holocaust, and the David Irving Trial* (Basic Books, 2001), 264–265.

degree of confidence about those actions what are we left with? It is not a matter of knowing with absolute certainty—for that is not possible in the realm of historical research. It is, however, a matter of knowing with a relative degree of confidence that Jesus existed, did what he did, and said what he said. It is a matter of having a degree of confidence that the Israelites were actually delivered from the Egyptians. Radical scepticism about knowing anything about the past is particularly destructive to the Christian faith.

V. A DEGREE OF CONFIDENCE

How do I know with confidence what has gone on before me? The following are a few things to consider when dealing with the questions surrounding historical objectivity, certainty and probability.

Probability, Not Logical (or absolute) Certainty

David Bebbington writes that historical knowledge is "always probable rather than certain."[5] This is important to remember, for we can expect a degree of certainty in disciplines such as chemistry or physics that is greater than we can expect in history. When seeking to reconstruct the past a historian has only evidence to interpret, and this evidence can never be incontrovertible. Historians are also influenced in their research by their own religious, political and cultural biases, biases that color their interpretation of the evidence. As in a court of law, this evidence is open to interpretation, and this evidence can only lead to a conclusion based on probability, not absolute certainty. In other words, there is no way to "prove" anything about the past (if by "prove" one means to come to a conclusion that is as certain as a conclusion in chemistry or physics). Rather, one must determine what happened by weighing evidence.

Lest you find this a bit depressing, note what Bebbington also says.[6] We could, he notes, doubt the existence of Pompey or Caesar (for

---

5. Bebbington, *Patterns in History*, 9.
6. Bebbington, *Patterns in History*, 9–10.

technically their existence is not absolutely certain). But, he argues, their existence is an "extremely strong" probability. He then provides the example of Richard Whately, *Historic Doubts Relative to Napoleon Buonaparte* (1819), a work of satire targeting Hume's denial of miracles. Whately's point, Bebbington concludes, is to show that any historical account is open to doubt, for we cannot be logically certain that they occurred. However, we accept that such events took place on the basis of probability, and in many cases it is highly probable that what we think happened actually happened.

Note that the distinction between "possible" and "probable" needs to be remembered. It may be possible that the Holocaust never happened (everyone could be lying, the pictures could be forgeries, the memories could be dreams or alien implants, and so on), but it is highly probable that it did. Possible is one thing, probable is another, and historians use evidence to construct probable accounts of past figures and events.

What about confidence and certainty regarding the past? The reality is that if you want absolute certainty in the same way a chemist wants absolute certainty, you will be disappointed and perhaps distressed. However, if you want confidence based on what is most probable, you should be able to sleep at night knowing that the past can be discovered with a degree of certainty.

Language Can Be Trusted (to a degree)

Contrary to the claims of some of the more radical deconstructionists, language can, to a degree, be trusted. The very fact that we (and even the deconstructionists) continue to converse and to write indicates that there is some form of communication taking place.[7] Regarding the trustworthiness of language, Mark Noll writes that the Bible contains statements about the "epistemic capacities" of humanity that lead to "confidence in the possibility of historical knowledge."[8] For example, it

---

7. Extreme postmodernism is self-refuting. See Evans, *In Defence of History*, 236–237.

8. Mark Noll, "A 'Peace of God'," *Books and Culture* (November/Decem-

is assumed in Scripture that people could know about God's actions in the present and in the past, and that people could know what one was saying (the ultimate example is the Incarnation, where God chose to enter into a particular culture and use that language to communicate with them, and with us, centuries later). However, before getting too dismissive of those who identify problems with language, note that Noll acknowledges that the Scriptures also speak of the influence of sin and its ability to distort and twist knowledge and our ability to know it.

A Postmodernist Approach Can Aid the Historian (to a degree)

Some of the questions and issues raised by postmodernists need to be remembered by historians. We should seek to hear from voices that have been ignored or suppressed. We should remember people have different perspectives on events, and these multiple perspectives need to be taken seriously.[9]

Good History Can Be Done

Despite the problems associated with historians (their biases) and the evidence (noted below in another chapter), good history can be done. One thing that I appreciate about Richard Evans' book *Lying About Hitler* is that it shows that bad research can be identified, good research can be done, and we can have a degree of confidence about what occurred in the past. The question in *Lying About Hitler* was whether or not David Irving was a Holocaust denier. In a court case over the issue it was shown over and over again that Irving did misuse primary sources (always with the same bent) and was, indeed, a Holocaust denier. Evans argues, and I agree, that this example vindicates the study of history: if normal conventions are used and integrity is the norm, then we can have some truth about the past. The following quote, though lengthy, summarizes this conclusion quite well:

---

ber 1999): 44.

    9. Evans is a critic of postmodernism, but even he sees some contributions from it. See Evans, *In Defence of History*, 243–249.

The trial taught the difference between real history and politically motivated propaganda. For truth, *The Guardian* rightly said, cannot be assumed, but 'has to be worked at . . . Even a casual reader of the case reports could quickly see how painstaking genuine historical scholarship is; it builds detail upon detail, avoiding casual inference and thin deduction.' It was truth established in this way over many years that had been vindicated. The trial demonstrated triumphantly the ability of historical scholarship to reach reasoned conclusions about the Nazi extermination of the Jews on the basis of a careful examination of the written evidence. It vindicated our capacity to know what happened after the survivors are no longer around to tell the tale. It showed that we *can* know, beyond reasonable doubt, even if explaining and understanding will always be a matter for debate.[10]

---

10. Evans, *Lying About Hitler*, 266.

7

The Sources

"Mine was the classic misadventure; I had wanted to master a source in order to confirm my youthful convictions; but it was finally the source that mastered me by imposing its own rhythms, its own chronology, and its own particular truth. My initial presuppositions had been stimulating, but they were now outmoded."

— Emmanuel Le Roy Ladurie

Historians make a distinction between primary and secondary sources.

- A *primary source* is from the time period being studied (e.g. a primary source in a study of the crusades is a eleventh-century sermon preached during the crusades).
- A *secondary source* is based on primary sources, but is compiled at a later date (e.g. a secondary source in a study of the crusades is what modern-day historians say about the crusades). In other words, original sources are considered primary sources, and what people said after the events described in the original sources are secondary sources.

One difficulty, however, is that the distinction between primary and secondary can get blurred at times. When does commentary on an event become a secondary and not a primary source? To use the example noted above, would a fifteenth-century history of the crusades be a primary source as well? What about eighteenth-century writings, or nineteenth-century writings? While the later writings are removed from the topic of study, what later commentators have stated can be helpful in determining how events were understood in the past. Despite these grey areas, historians must rely on primary sources for their access to the past; to do otherwise is to be even further removed from what is being studied.

I. PRIMARY SOURCES

A. Types of Primary Sources

Historians work with evidence that makes a link to the past. In other words, anything that provides information about the past is a source for historians and their research. Some sources are more obvious than others, some more numerous, and some more easy to decipher. Nevertheless, historians look at any source that provides clues to the past. The following are some of the types of sources that historians look at.

Artefacts

Dates and inscriptions on a tombstone remind subsequent generations of a few key details of a deceased loved one. A ruined baptismal tank and a scattering of stones from the walls of a once majestic cathedral remind us of a previously beautiful building. Coins, buildings, statues, paintings, and jewellery provide glimpses of past cultures. Monuments, weapons, battlefields, and uniforms inform us of impressive victories and martial glory. Scratchings on the walls of dungeons by emaciated and doomed prisoners provide a different view of the past from the perspective of the oppressed. Even today's movies will be artefacts for future generations of historians interested in twenty-first-century popular culture. Anything that remains from the past is a link to the past, and such artefacts can be used to help reconstruct the past.

Written Documents

The most common artefacts that historians use to reconstruct the past are written documents that have somehow survived the ravages of time. Remember, for something carved into stone to survive is one thing, for something written on paper it is quite another.[1] Mould, fire (accidental and intentional), tears, hungry bugs, water damage and myriad other threats make it difficult for any paper to survive throughout the centuries. Professional modern climate-controlled archives are important, but even the most modern conservation attempts only slow down decay, not stop it completely.

There are many different types of written documents, and to name them all here would be impossible. However, the following is a list of written sources that would be common for historians of Christianity to use.

- Official Public Documents: creeds, council decisions, synod/presbytery decisions, denominational decisions or statements, papal decrees, policy statements, doctrinal formulations.
- Published Documents: hymn books, denominational publications (newspapers, newsletters, brochures), books, autobiographies, sermons.
- Unpublished Documents:[2] journals, diaries, letters, minutes from various meetings, baptismal records, birth records, and marriage records.

---

1. Of course, documents were also written on other items such as ostraca (broken pieces of pottery) and animal skins.

2. Note that unpublished sources such as journals or diaries often do not survive as well as published or official documents. Why? Someone usually tries to preserve official documents. Note also that some journals or diaries were written with future readers (or even publication) in mind.

The value of written sources cannot be underestimated. As Tosh notes, from the High Middle Ages (c. 1000 AD) onwards the written word is the most abundant source for historians, and usually the most helpful in providing a detailed knowledge of the past. It is no surprise, then, that historians usually go first (and sometimes only) to such sources.[3]

Oral Accounts

Another type of source is that of an oral account. While less common today (especially in the West), in many cultures oral accounts have played an important part in the preservation and transmission of the past. Some oral accounts go back generations, whereas an oral account may be as simple as someone telling about their experience of a twenty-year-old church split. For pastors going into churches, oral accounts of the past are often more authoritative than any written document!

One last comment about sources is in order. Most sources are created by those in positions of power: the educated elite or the official authorities (usually one and the same) who could write and who had official sanction from those in power. A recent trend in historical research has been to focus on hearing the voices of the powerless, or the "common people." When identifying sources try to get a sense of what voice you are listening to, and how you can get at other voices to provide a broader picture of events. For instance, a minister's sermon on prohibition published in a denominational newspaper provides one perspective, a lay person's journal entry on the same issue may present a very different perspective. The point being made here is not that one source is necessarily better or worse than another, it just needs to be asked by the researcher what voice(s) is speaking in the source.

---

3. John Tosh, *The Pursuit of History: Aims, Methods and New Directions in the Study of Modern History* (London/New York: Longman, 1991), 31–32.

B. Finding Primary Sources

The movie character Indiana Jones has made finding artefacts appear to be a fascinating and deadly enterprise. While church archival work may not be as dangerous (lots of dust, but few snakes!), it is fascinating and rewarding for those who love the study of the past.

Professional historians spend a great deal of time in archives locating and analyzing primary sources.[4] Most seminary students, however, will not have to visit an archives to complete their course work. Instead, they will probably use either a published sourcebook of primary sources, Internet primary sources, or a combination of the two. These types of prepared sources (usually translated into English) make life much easier and the past more accessible for students.

Before going further, here is a brief note to those who will become pastors in local churches. Your church building will contain a wide variety of primary sources: official documents, published documents and unpublished documents, as well as oral accounts. In fact, the building itself is a very large artefact. You would be wise to "read" the sources around you so as to discern the past. You would also help subsequent generations if you did all you could to preserve such sources.

C. Handling the Primary Sources

For students who are using published sourcebooks or the Internet, there is no need to be cautious about damaging a valuable treasure from the past. For those going into archives there is a protocol that should be followed:

- Use a pencil
- Do not handle anything old without cloth gloves (usually provided by archives)
- Treat material with extreme care

---

4. Most denominations, or presbyteries, synods or other official structures, have an archives.

- No food or drinks near material
- Do not write on anything
- Do not re-file anything (unless instructed otherwise)

These are just common guidelines. It is wise to check on local protocol, privacy and copyright issues with each local archives.[5]

D. The Problems of Primary Sources

There are a variety of difficulties related to primary sources, some of the generalized and theoretical ones are dealt with in the chapter above on objectivity. In this section, some specific problems associated with primary sources will be outlined.

Bebbington writes that the problem with primary sources is at least a threefold one: time, number and reliability.[6] In regards to *time,* the evidence is often quite old and far removed from the present. This distance makes the task of the historian unique from other disciplines that have their object of study right before them. Some of the problems associated with time include language differences (can you read ninth-century Russian?), cultural differences (what were the assumptions in the tenth-century Byzantine Empire that we today do not understand?), political differences (what were the political pressures that necessitated the start of the crusades in the eleventh century?) and religious differences (why were pilgrimages so important for the thirteenth-century Western European Christian?). Usually the further back one goes in time the harder it is to overcome the problems associated with time. However, that is not always the case. Due to a relative abundance of sources we know more about first-century Roman life than we do of fourth-century Germanic life outside of the empire. The problem of time can be minimized by learning the necessary language(s) and

---

5. For a humorous example of what can go wrong when dealing with a priceless ancient book, see the Mr. Bean episode entitled "The Library".

6. Bebbington, *Patterns in History,* 3–5.

unique aspects of the period in which the source is located, but even the most diligent study will never entirely eliminate the problem of time.

The problem of *number* is a problem related to the number of resources available. There is never enough evidence to gain a complete picture of the past. Sometimes the problem of number is that there was simply not enough written about the particular event. Many church meetings have summaries of decisions, but no material on why and how the decisions were reached. For instance, a contentious three-hour board meeting can often be summarized in two sentences, or a two-month council meeting can produce a summary of decisions, but nothing more. In these cases, more material would have provided us with supplementary information that could help answer questions that we have about past decisions. Sometimes the problem of number is different in that some sources that did at one time exist have gone missing (accidentally or otherwise), and as a result we have an incomplete record of events. In these cases historians can keep looking for sources to "fill in the missing gaps," but in the meantime have to make somewhat tentative decisions. An even more difficult aspect of the problem of number is when there is absolutely nothing (at least as far as we know) recorded about an event or person.

The evidence is also not always *reliable*. The historian cannot assume that "just because something is written down" it is true. As noted above, historians always try to get at primary sources. But even when they do get their hands on a primary source, historians are well aware that it may not be a trustworthy source. The reasons for a document being untrustworthy can be divided into two main categories: intentional and unintentional. Intentional inaccuracies can be as malevolent as forgery, slander, lying, or can be as innocent as a passionate and loyal description of a hero that intentionally excludes anything that does not reflect positively on the hero (e.g. the worst excesses of hagiography). Within this category of reliability could also be editorial interventions that omit a particular side of a debate. One even needs to read personal journals or diaries with a critical eye, for some write those documents with an eye on future readers and can be written in such a way as to include or exclude information accordingly. An extreme example of the unreliability of sources is that of various Soviet histories that skewed the history of the Soviet Union. Recognizing the unreliability of these histories, the Soviet Union's leader Gorbachev banned the reading of Soviet history in high schools, and then cancelled national high school exams because there "was not point in testing the student's knowledge of lies."[7] One term to remember is "provenance." This term refers to the origins of the source. Can the source be traced back to its origins? In other words, can it be trusted to be authentic? Unintentional inaccuracies are caused by a wide variety of reasons. One needs to be alert for recording, spelling, and translating mistakes. Eyewitness accounts can be accurate in the opinion of the person who saw the event, but everyone knows that although eyewitness accounts of the same traffic accident agree on many points (e.g. the cars collided, it was raining), they often disagree about other factors (e.g. whose fault it was, how fast the cars were going). Consequently, eyewitness accounts need to be considered carefully and be corroborated from other sources as much as possible.

Due to these problems with sources historians must approach the evidence with a healthy degree of scepticism and a critical mind. Every source must be challenged and authenticated, every claim must be weighed, and every conclusion supported by the best evidence at hand. Of course, even in the most ideal situation there is never enough material written to record absolutely every action and thought. There is also the grim reality that external actions are often recorded, but internal thoughts and feelings are not. It may be relatively easy to get at what people did, but very problematic to get at why they did it. Despite these limitations, and because of these limitations, historians must pore over primary sources to get the best possible evidence for their claims about the past. It is this "struggle with the documents" that

---

7.   See Joyce Appleby, Lynn Hunt and Margaret Jacob, *Telling the Truth About History* (New York/London: W.W. Norton & Company, 1994), 290.

separates the professional historian from the amateur,[8] and you need to do all that you can to enter into this struggle.

E. Making Sense of the Primary Sources

While searching through primary sources can be an enjoyable (although sometimes daunting) experience, a pile of notes and material at the end of the process presents a problem. How do you make sense of your sources? If you have a thesis, you will need to marshal an argument based predominantly on primary sources. If not, you can use the sources to illustrate any points you are trying to make. The following examples related to the Roman Emperor Constantine should illustrate the difference.

Purpose of assignment	Example	Use of primary sources	Example
Thesis	This paper argues that Emperor Constantine called the Council of Nicaea (325 A.D.) due to concerns about political unity in the empire.	Use as evidence to prove a point.	Any sources that substantiate your claim would be used. (Note—if the evidence goes counter to your thesis you will need to change your thesis!)
No thesis	This paper provides a summary of Constantine's life.	Use as illustrative material to provide a well-rounded and interesting portrayal of the man.	Any sources that provide some examples of his life or convictions would be used.

---

8. Marc Bloch as quoted by Tosh, *The Pursuit of History*, 57.

Of course, knowing one's purpose ahead of time will make the search process easier and more efficient. Once the material has been gathered, then it is organized and presented to complete the assignment.

F. Types of Questions to Ask

The following questions are the sorts of questions you should ask of any primary source:

- What is the document's (or artefact's) provenance? Can it be trusted?
- What significant social, political, personal and theological factors influenced the author?
- Who was the author?
- What was the author's purpose in writing? Who was his/her audience?
- Whose voice is not being heard in this text?
- What was most important to the author?
- What difference would it make if you could read the document in the original language?
- What are key words or themes?
- What was the author's and audience's emotional/political/ social state?
- To what authorities did the author appeal?
- What were the author's basic assumptions that influenced his/ her writing?
- What role was the state to play?
- How is the "Other" being constructed? (and for what reason?)[9]
- Is this document a full statement of the author's beliefs, or would reading other writings of the author reveal more? Are there other writings? Did the author change his/her mind at a later date?

---

9. See Chapter Eight for a discussion of the creation of the "Other."

- Do the author's conclusions contradict or support "received" views on the topic?
- What does this say about what happened, and what does this say about why it happened?

II. SECONDARY SOURCES

Up to this point I have emphasized primary sources. However, secondary source materials are key for any study of history. Based on primary sources and the conclusions of other secondary sources, these materials are historians' attempts at explaining and understanding the past. They also provide the helpful "big picture" for any reading of primary sources. For example, a reading of John Wesley's personal journals will tell us a great deal about his daily affairs, his convictions and contacts, as well as other aspects of the birth of evangelicalism. However, if we want to understand Wesley in the broader religious, social, political and economic context of the eighteenth century we will need to read other texts. If we want to know what others have said about Wesley based on their research we will also need to go to secondary source material. (It is always embarrassing to claim that your research is original when others have done the same thing before. Check first before making grand claims!)

The conclusions in secondary sources, of course, must not be automatically accepted as correct. It is always helpful to compare the results of one secondary source with another secondary source. Ask why they agree, or why they disagree. You also need to ask critical questions of any secondary sources that you use. Just as men and women in the past had biases or were under certain pressures, so are modern historians. For example, in a study of the Reformation you should determine if the author is Catholic or Protestant. Such loyalties may, or may not, impact the slant or bias of the author.

One important term to remember is periodization. This term refers to the way in which historians categorize or group matters. It is a generalized description that is meant to explain a period, movement, actions, or ideas. The purpose of periodization is to make sense of the past. The advantage of periodization is that it helps us understand patterns and generalized behaviours. The danger of periodization is that it can cause us to look at the past through the way in which it has been periodized rather than by the way it actually was.

8

The Historian

*"The historian should be fearless and incorruptible; a man
of independence, loving frankness and truth; one who, as the
poets says, calls a fig a fig and a spade a spade. He should
yield to neither hatred nor affection, nor should be unsparing
and unpitying. He should be neither shy nor deprecating,
but an impartial judge, giving each side all it deserves but
no more. He should know in his writing no country and no
city; he should bow to no authority and acknowledge no
king. He should never consider what this or that man will
think, but should state the facts as they really occurred."*

— Lucian

The problems associated with primary sources are compounded by
what historians bring to the interpretive process. Every historian
has a predisposition to one opinion or the other, and this predisposition
profoundly impacts judgment in areas such as the selection of materials,
how to structure material, and how to interpret sources. The following
is a discussion of the dynamics surrounding the historian's intentions,
biases, integrity, theories and limitations.

Before I go on, however, remember that the following comments
apply equally to professional historians and non-professionals alike,
even in the local church context. Everyone in ministry will need to
think like an historian at one time or another. Why did that family

decide to leave the church? Why did the church split ten years ago? Who said what at the annual meeting two years ago? Have we grown numerically in the past twenty years? When did our local church begin? How these types of question will be answered is impacted by the predisposition of the researcher.

I. INTENTIONS

One very important question to ask is "what were the historian's intentions"? Knowing the answer to this question is important, for the intention of the historian can shape the focus of the study and also skew the conclusions reached. For instance, the sixteenth-century German reformer Martin Luther used church history to challenge Roman Catholic tradition (e.g., the papacy was the result of historical developments, for the early church was run by councils and other means). To bolster the Protestant cause of the Reformation in England, Robert Barnes (c. 1495–1540) wrote *Lives of Roman Pontiffs* in order to show the many disreputable and sinful actions of past Popes. In response to these types of criticisms, the papacy commissioned Caesar Boronius to write *Ecclesiastic Annals* that defended the Medieval theological developments in the church as legitimate interpretations of Scripture and manifestations of the Holy Spirit's work. Obviously the intentions of these historians affected what sources they looked at, how they interpreted them, and what they concluded.

At a local church level, remember that intentions certainly impact how people interpret the history of your local church. For instance, the group involved in the pressure put on the last pastor to leave has a vested interest in portraying the pastor as a problem, while those loyal to the ousted pastor have a passionate commitment to portraying the pastor as competent and unjustly treated by rebellious troublemakers.

There are many reasons why people write about the past. Your job is to ask yourself what your reasons are, or what the reasons of others are, and how these reasons have shaped the research conclusions.

II. BIASES

This is closely related to the above-mentioned issue of intentions (of course, the intention of the research is very much a bias). However, there are other related obvious and not-so-obvious biases that have an effect on the way in which research unfolds:

- Sources (e.g., why one source over another?)
- People (e.g., why one person over another?)
- Period (e.g., why one century over another?)
- Culture (e.g., why one culture over another?)
- Group (e.g., why Protestant instead of Orthodox? why powerful instead of powerless? why male instead of female? why adult instead of child?)
- Language (e.g., why French instead of Latin?)

One last assumption that requires special attention is that of race. Edward Said has shown how racial assumptions about the Orient influenced two centuries of writing about "Orientalism."[1] Postcolonial works have built upon his conclusions, and now historians are much more sensitive to how assumptions about race impact our perceptions about the past, and how we can create an "Other" that reflects more our assumptions and prejudices rather than anything about the actual person or event being studied. Look for this when reading, and watch for this when writing.

III. THEORIES

Closely related to biases are commitments to a particular theory or methodology. There are many theories that historians bring to the task of research as a way of helping them understand the past. Marxist

---

1. Edward Said's *Orientalism* (New York: Vintage Books, 1979) is a "classic" in postcolonial studies.

historians look at the economic factors that contributed to particular events and beliefs. For instance, they would look at the economic or material reasons for why a person joined in the crusades. On the one hand, such a theory may be helpful in bringing to light some aspects of the past, for no doubt there were economic factors involved in such decisions. On the other hand, the theory may actually hinder getting at the past if the theory is superimposed on the past, and reduces the past to one factor or one dimension. While the crusader may have had material motives, what about spiritual motives to sign up and fight in the east? How would a focus on the material keep us from seeing this aspect of a soldier's zeal? Historians must let the past speak for itself, and not superimpose modern theories or pre-conceptions upon it.

IV. INTEGRITY

It is quite natural for historians to be so focused on their research and their methodological assumptions that they refuse to consider evidence that goes against the grain of their own convictions. What makes it even more tempting is the fact that most people do not go to archives to check on other people's interpretation of primary sources. However, honest scholarship and Christian integrity means including evidence that fits and does not fit your thesis.

The temptation to fudge on details is greater on biographical research of a hero, or on a dark part of the church's history such as the Inquisition. You may not like what you find in your research, but it needs to be noted nonetheless. Of course, another form of dishonesty is to present material out of context or out of proportion. I often say that student writing must avoid two extreme genres: extreme hagiography (did everything right) and supermarket checkout store magazines (sensationalistic digging up nothing but dirt). Perspective, context and honesty are required when sifting through evidence. Let the text speak for itself. Even if the author's comments are shocking, disagreeable, or you even consider them heretical, your role as an historian is not to correct what is there, but merely to discover what was said or done. You certainly are entitled to your opinion about the rightness or wrongness of what you discover, but the first task of the historian is to study the text itself and to let it speak for itself.

V. LIMITATIONS

Every historian has limitations, and these limitations affect research. The following is a list of these limitations: note that some are imposed upon on the historian, and may be overcome quite simply (more money and time for travel) or with more work (learn a new language).

- Geography (e.g., sources are too far to get to)
- Language (e.g., sources are in a foreign language)
- Time (e.g., other demands may mean that the research was rushed or could not be as comprehensive as desired)
- Access (e.g., sources are incomplete, or access to sources was denied for some reason)
- Skill (e.g., just like there are good mechanics and poor mechanics, there are good historians and poor historians)
- Humanity (e.g., peeple maykes mistukes—inclueding history-ians)

In conclusion, you can see that there are many factors that impact the historian's ability to be impartial. This conclusion does not mean that historians cannot be trusted, or that attempts to know the past are futile. What it does mean is that we must rigorously apply ourselves to identifying and minimizing our own present prejudices and weakness at the same time as we critically analyze the primary sources from the past.

9

Types of Assignments

"Faithfulness to the truth of history involves far more than a research, however patient and scrupulous, into special facts. Such facts may be detailed with the most minute exactness, and yet the narrative, taken as a whole, may be unmeaning or untrue. The narrator must seek to imbue himself with the life and spirit of the time. He must study events in their bearings near and remote; in the character, habits, and manners of those who took part in them. He must himself be, as it were, a sharer or a spectator of the action he describes."

— Francis Parkman

There are many types of ways in which historical research is carried out. The following types of assignments are some of the more common ones in Christian history courses at seminary. Each type of assignment is unique, and has a specific intended outcome.

I. BOOK REVIEW

What is a book review?

In the most basic sense, a book review is a review of a book's contents. By contents, however, more is meant than just the author's thesis (as important as that is). A good book review also includes commentary on the sources used, the outline (breakdown of chapters), any theory(s) that shaped the interpretation and organization of sources, as well as a statement on the book's value and unique contribution. Some reviews have an element of your reaction to, or reflection on, the contents. In those cases, the shift is away from a more rigid summary and critique of the contents to a personal interaction with the book.

Why do professors give this assignment?

A book review accomplishes a few important things. First, it provides students with a detailed and comprehensive knowledge of the topic of the book. Class lectures are important, but reading a book in its entirety provides a deeper level of information than can be provided in class (it may also provide a way of dealing with information not covered in class). Second, students often just dip into books to get "facts" for papers. This is okay, but there are times when an entire book needs to be read, and this assignment requires students to do just that. Third, learning to read a book and grasp the author's overall thesis and way of arguing for it are important skills to develop in any discipline. A book review will aid in the development of these skills.

How can one do well?

As with anything, writing a good book review takes work and practice. The following are some key things to remember when writing a review. First and foremost, read the book! Avoid trying to review a book that you have not read, for not only do you miss out on the information contained in the book, but also your assignment (and grade!) will suffer. In regards to expectations, get clarification from the professor as to what type of review is expected (especially in regards to any personal reflection). It is also wise to see if there have been any other reviews of the book. These other reviews should be read for guidance, but make sure your review is your review (and do not forget to document your use of other reviews). In an ideal world, you would have time to get a feel for the subject matter and be able to place the book within the larger context of other books on the same subject matter. If you can do this (even in the most basic sense) all the better.

II. BIOGRAPHICAL PAPER

What is a biographical paper?

A biographical paper is a summary of a person's life, thought and impact. The paper may or may not have a thesis.

No Thesis

A biographical paper with no thesis focuses on a more general answering of a variety of questions. When you write the paper try to answer the five w's: *who* was he/she, *when* did he/she live, *where* did he/she live, *what* did he/she do, *why* is he/she "famous" and why should we learn about him/her? Also of concern for the historian is *how* we know about the person, and *why* there are different interpretations of a person's life/actions.

Thesis

A biographical paper with a thesis sets out to argue something very specific about a person (rather than focusing on outlining the person's entire life). For instance, it may be that you want to argue that Pope Urban II's concern for the crusades was an attempt to bolster his own power back in Europe, or that Billy Graham's success was due to his superior organizational ability. Whatever the case, a biographical paper with a thesis needs to address and answer a specific question.

Why do professors give this assignment?

People make history, and biographical papers are attempts to research these people. Biographical research can often be more interesting than looking at movements, events or ideas. People can also be more controversial, and getting at why someone did something can provoke a variety of responses from supporters and opponents!

How can one do well?

There are a few things to keep in mind when doing this type of research. First, avoid hagiography. No one is perfect, so do not be afraid of identifying warts and all. (Of course, be fair and avoid just focusing on the warts.) A good biographical paper will note what different historians have said about the person, and there are always divergent positions on people (even saintly Mother Teresa has her critics!). Second, get access to primary sources and read them. If your paper is on Francis of Assisi, read what he wrote. It is not always possible or practical to read everything written by the person, but you should read something. Access to primary sources is important, and make sure that you quote the person in your paper. Third, seek to understand the person in his/her context. It is easy to judge, but far harder to understand.

III. RESEARCH PAPER

What is a research paper?

Research papers are just that: research. A research paper requires students to delve into the taxing art and discipline of research, and is usually concerned with arguing a thesis. Research papers require students to discover, compile, critique, analyze and synthesize the conclusions of sources and scholars so that a period, person, movement or theme is studied or that a question is answered.

No Thesis

If a research paper on a particular period, person, movement or theme does not require a thesis there is still work to be done. For instance, if the research is on the sixteenth-century Reformation it is necessary to not only get your hands on the writings of some sixteenth-century reformers (these sources would provide some helpful eyewitness accounts of events), but also find sources that explain the origin, birth, events and outcome of the Reformation. Such an assignment also seeks to identify key Reformation people, writings, theology and issues. Of course, divergent views of the Reformation also need to be identified. The end result of such research is a paper that gave a thoughtful and comprehensive view of the Reformation.

Thesis

In its most basic sense, a thesis is something that the paper is attempting to argue and defend. In the discipline of history primary sources play a key role in the argument of a thesis. In other words, one's thesis must ultimately be able to be sustained from the primary sources.

A paper that requires a thesis must argue something; a general summary of a period, person, movement or theme is not enough. As much as possible primary sources must be used in the argument, and secondary sources must be included to supply an interpretive or methodological framework as well as necessary background information. In all cases the argument (or thesis) is clearly stated and argued; the rest of the paper makes a case for the thesis by providing evidence and analysis. It also takes to task those scholars who have argued differently. See the chart below for some examples of a progression to a thesis.

Why do professors give this assignment?

There are a variety of reasons why research papers are important. Research that does not require a thesis provides students with a chance for a thoughtful, but general, study of a period, person, movement or theme of interest. Thesis driven research provides the opportunity to answer some questions that naturally arise from a study of a period, person, movement or theme. For instance, why did German Lutheranism not spread in France, or why did people join the First Crusade? The answer to these questions is a thesis. A thesis moves beyond just a chronicle or description of the past to an explanation of the past.

How can one do well?

The most basic thing is to make sure that you have a thesis if the research requires a thesis. State the thesis in the opening paragraph, or at least the first page. Try to avoid straying from the thesis. Whether or not the research has a thesis, make sure you include important primary sources, relevant secondary sources, and note any areas of disagreement among historians.

RESEARCH SUBJECT AREA	FORM A QUESTION	DEVELOP A THESIS	ARGUE & DEFEND
Study a period, person, movement or theme. The more you know of a particular subject area the more able you will be to come up with a question.	Ask a question based on your study.	Develop an answer to your question based on the evidence.	Anticipate what others will ask of the thesis, and marshal arguments to deal with questions. Be open to changing your thesis if evidence warrants.
A study of the birth and spread of the Protestant Reformation.	*Why did German Lutheranism not spread in France?*	*This paper argues that German Lutheranism did not spread in France because Lutheranism appeared too German.* *What primary and secondary source evidence is there to support this thesis?*	*What other reason(s) could have been a factor? What about Dr. Smith who argues for some other reason?*
A study of the crusades.	*Why did people join the First Crusade?*	*This paper argues that people joined the First Crusade primarily for religious reasons.* *What primary and secondary source evidence is there to support this thesis?*	*What other reason(s) could have been a factor? What about the Marxist Dr. Jones who argues that they fought mainly for material gain?*
A study of the Roman Emperor Constantine.	*Was his conversion to Christianity authentic?*	*This paper argues that Constantine was never really converted, and that his conversion was a politically motivated ruse.* *What primary and secondary source evidence is there to support this thesis?*	*What other reason(s) could have been a factor? What about Dr. Kazinsky who argues that his conversion was real?*

10

Documentation

"Slow and steady, steady and slow, that's the only way to go."

— Goofy (from one of my children's storybooks)

While this brief chapter may be the most brief and boring of all, proper documentation often makes or breaks a research project. This chapter will provide you with the basics of what history professors look for when evaluating your research. Of course, many schools have their own "in house" style guide, so check with your professor for specific expectations in regards to documentation.

I. DOCUMENTING THE PRIMARY SOURCES

It is very important to document your discoveries. Could you, or someone else, go back and easily find the information? Whether or not you are digging in archives, using the Internet or searching in your sourcebook, you need to pay attention to documentation. At the very least you need to identify the author, date, place, reason why created (profit, personal use, political goals, end controversy, etc.), genre, audience, mode of publication, provenance, and later editing (if so, by whom, for what, when, how?). Historians have a variety of systems for documentation, so find one that you are comfortable with and will be able to both help you find things again and assist you in the organization of your research.

II. FOOTNOTE & ENDNOTES

Historical writing uses footnotes or endnotes for documentation. Remember to check your particular school's style guide.

III. BIBLIOGRAPHY

Note that the bibliography of a history assignment should always be divided into two sections: primary and secondary sources. Primary sources should be listed first, followed by secondary sources. This breakdown allows readers to make a quick assessment of what was used for original sources. Normal rules of alphabetical order by last name apply within the two subheadings.

IV. TENSE

Because your paper often refers to the past and the present it is easy to get mixed up. It is usually best to refer to the past in past tense: Martin Luther *said*, Joan of Arc *went*, Pope Innocent III *did*, makes more sense than Martin Luther *says*, Joan of Arc *goes*, Pope Innocent III *does*. The really important thing is that you do not go back and forth with tense. For instance, avoid Pope Innocent III *said* and then on another page Pope Innocent III *says*.

V. AD VS CE

For over a thousand years dating in the West was decidedly Christian in that everything was dated before Christ (BC) or after Christ (AD, *Anno Domini* "in the year of our Lord"). This fixation on the coming of Christ was more than a matter of convenience, but a core theological conviction: Jesus Christ's coming was at the center of human history and God's plan for it. As Kenneth Scott Latourette notes: "To the Christian, however, this reckoning of time is much more than a convention. It is inherent in history. In Jesus of Nazareth, so the Christian holds,

God once for all disclosed Himself and acted decisively."[1] However, in today's rapidly secularizing and de-Christianizing West there is a move away from using this distinctly Christian form of dating. The new (and supposedly inclusive) way to date events is to use BCE (Before Common Era) or CE (Common Era). Note that events are still dated before and after Christ—it is just that this is not to be mentioned. You should check with your professors to see what they want for their assignments. Of course, you also need to think about whether or not you agree with using the traditional AD or the new CE.

---

1.   Kenneth Scott Latourette, "The Christian Understanding of History," in *God, History, and Historians: An Anthology of Modern Christian Views of History,* ed. C.T. McIntire (New York: Oxford University Press, 1977), 53.

CONCLUSION

Death, taxes and church history is a potent and fearful triumvirate. On the one hand, church history should remain on that list for, as Colin Brown notes, it cannot be avoided: "We cannot get away from history any more than a fish swimming in the sea can get away from the water. Human beings live in history. History no less than nature forms our environment. Things that happened in the past affect the course of the present."[1] On the other hand, does church history have to be as painful as taxes and as feared as death? I think not.

The study of the church's history is an important part of any seminary's curriculum. It can also be an enjoyable and meaningful part of everyone's involvement in ministry. You do not have to be a professional historian to do well in your courses. All that is needed is a commitment to the basic principles outlined in this book. While I hope that you do well in your courses, I also desire that your courses instil in you a desire to continue to study the church's history. The benefits of such study should readily become apparent, for as Jean Bodin stated "'The study of History is the beginning of wisdom.'"

---

1.   Brown, *History and Faith*, 37.

Bibliography

The following is a brief bibliography of books that I recommend for further reading. There are numerous books that could be added to this list, but I have selected the following because I have personally found them to be particularly helpful for one reason or another. Note that some of the following are overtly Christian, and others not at all.

BRIEF INTRODUCTIONS TO THE DISCIPLINE OF HISTORY

Bloch, Marc. *The Historian's Craft*. New York: Alfred A. Knopf, 1963.

Tosh, John. *The Pursuit of History: Aims, Methods and New Directions in the Study of Modern History*. London/New York: Longman, 1991.

CHRISTIAN VIEWS OF HISTORY

St. Augustine. *City of God*.

Bebbington, David. *Patterns in History: A Christian Perspective on Historical Thought*. Leicester: Apollos, 1990.

Bradley, James E. and Richard A. Muller. *Church History: An Introduction to Research, Reference Works, and Methods*. Grand Rapids: Eerdmans, 1995.

Brown, Colin. *History and Faith: A Personal Exploration*. Grand Rapids: Zondervan, 1987.

Butterfield, Herbert. *Christianity and History*. Fontana, 1957.

Eusebius. *Ecclesiastical History*.

Marsden, George and Frank Roberts, eds. *A Christian View of History?* Grand Rapids: Eerdmans, 1975.

McIntire, C.T., ed. *God, History, and Historians: An Anthology of Modern Christian Views of History*. New York: Oxford University Press, 1977.

McIntire, C.T. and Ronald A. Wells, eds. *History and Historical Understanding*. Grand Rapids: Eerdmans, 1984.

Montgomery, John Warwick. *Where is History Going?: A Christian Response to Secular Philosophies of History*. Minneapolis: Bethany House, 1969.

A conversation with George Marsden and John Woodbridge on combining Christian convictions with scholarly conventions. "Christian History Today." *Christian History* 20/4 (2001): 50-54.

HISTORIOGRAPHY

Bauman, Michael and Martin L Klauber, eds. *Historians of the Christian Tradition: Their Methodology and Influence on Western Thought*. Nashville: Broadman & Holman Publishers, 1995.

Breisach, Ernst. *Historiography: Ancient, Medieval, and Modern* (2nd ed.). University of Chicago Press, 1994.

Gilderhus, Mark T. *History and Historians: A Historiographical Introduction* (5th ed.). Upper Saddle River: Prentice Hall, 2003.

Wilson, Norman J. *History in Crisis? Recent Directions in Historiography*. Upper Saddle River, NJ: Prentice Hall, 1999.

MODERN ISSUES: POSTMODERNISM, DECONSTRUCTIONISM, POSTCOLONIALISM, OBJECTIVITY

Appleby, Joyce, Lynn Hunt and Margaret Jacob. *Telling the Truth About History*. New York/London: W.W. Norton & Company, 1994.

Chaves, Jonathan. "Soul and Reason in Literary Criticism: Deconstructing the Deconstructionists." *Journal of American Oriental Society (2002): 828-835.*

Curthoys, Ann and John Docker, *Is History Fiction?* Ann Arbor: University of Michigan Press, 2005.

Evans, Richard. *In Defence of History*. London: Granta Books, 1997.

Evans, Richard. *Lying About Hitler: History, Holocaust, and the David Irving Trial*. Basic Books, 2001.

Noll, Mark A. "Traditional Christianity and the Possibility of Historical Knowledge." *Christian Scholar's Review* 19/4 (1990): 388-406.

Novick, Peter. *That Noble Dream: The "Objectivity Question" and the American Historical Profession*. Cambridge: Cambridge University Press, 1988.

Stone, Dan. *Constructing the Holocaust: A Study in Historiography*. London/Portland: Vallentine Mitchell, 2003.

REFLECTIONS ON THE STUDY OF HISTORY

Bainton, Roland. *Yesterday, Today, and What Next?* Minneapolis: Augsburg Publishing House, 1978.

Durant, Will and Ariel Durant. *The Lessons of History*. New York: Simon and Schuster, 1968.

Hindmarsh, Bruce D. "On Not Forgetting the Story of the Church." *Crux* 40/4 (December 2004): 2-9.

Williams, Rowan. *Why Study the Past? The Quest for the Historical Church*. Grand Rapids: Eerdmans, 2005.

Glossary of Terms

Anachronistic
To be anachronistic is to take modern day perceptions or conceptions and impose them on a past period or person. For instance, to look for or expect twenty-first century conceptions of women in the ninth century is unfair and anachronistic. Each period (or person) should be understood in its own context.

Extant
A term to describe a source that has survived to the present day.

Hagiography
Technically writing of the saints (*hagios* = holy and *graphos* = writing), but the term usually refers to a genre filled with uncritical praise for a person or movement. For example, to write about a saint's holiness, miracles and amazing decisions, without ever asking critical questions about actions or ideas, is to engage in hagiography.

Historiography
A study of the study of history. Historiography is concerned with problems (and possibilities) associated with critical theories, sources, and the ways in which historians have constructed arguments.

Primary Source
A primary source is from the time period being studied (e.g., a primary source in a study of the crusades is a eleventh-century sermon preached during the crusades).

Secondary Source
A secondary source is based on primary sources, but is compiled at a later date (e.g. a secondary source in a study of the crusades is what modern-day historians say about the crusades). In other words, original sources are considered primary sources, and what people said after the events described in the original sources are secondary sources.

Periodization
The way in which a period is characterized. It is like a reputation that colors everything about a period. For instance, a Protestant history may characterize the Roman Catholic Church as totally corrupt and far removed from the gospel. However, such a portrayal (e.g. periodization) blinds people to seeing the renewal movements that were going on in Catholicism before, during and after the Reformation. Periodization can be helpful, but just be careful that it is not keeping you from seeing something.

Provenance
A term used to describe the history of a particular source. For instance, to know a document's, or artifact's, provenance is to know the origins of the source and how it has survived to the present day (you may never know everything, but you may know enough to give you confidence). The critical issue is reliability: to know the provenance of the source may give you more or less confidence in that particular piece of evidence.

Thesis
A thesis is an argument. A typical history research paper has a thesis; in other words, the paper must argue something based on the evidence.

Teleology

An approach to history that sees patterns and trends that lead towards a forgone conclusion. Whether the end is an apocalypse, worker's revolt, democratic reform, or whatever, teleology is the term to describe an historian's perspective that interprets the past as one big series of events that have led to the grand event. Any other possible options seem to be ignored—all history is moving towards the grand event.

The Other

A term to describe how a people or person has been constructed. Edward Said is the main figure associated with this term. Whenever you are looking at how someone has been constructed you should always ask why is that person being constructed in that manner. Is it racism? Fear? Hatred? Imperial ideology? Or some other reason?

Chronicle

A chronicle that simply describes what happened (e.g., dates, names, events) is usually contrasted with a history. While there is some interpretation in the chronicler's selection of dates, a history usually provides criticism, interpretation and synthesis with other conclusions reached by other scholars.

APPENDIX B

Using Church History in Church

The following are some suggestions for introducing church history into your local church's life and ministry.

Sermon Series
There are a few options for this type of history from the pulpit. You can offer a sermon series on a particular period or theme such as the Reformation, the growth of the early church, key moments, etc. You could also offer a biographical sermon on an important figure. A unique, but challenging, variation on a biographical sermon is to get dressed up and act as if you are the person (this is risky and takes time and skill—but is rewarding if done right). Another variation on this is to preach an actual sermon written by the historical figure.

Sunday School
Rather than offer another Bible study, why not offer an elective on an historical topic? A survey of the church's history, or of a particular period, person or issue, would be good options.

Hymn History

Why not spend a few minutes introducing the history of a hymn (or hymn writer) before singing the hymn? Knowing the setting of the hymn often adds a powerful dimension to the singing of it. Another variation of this idea is to have a service devoted to outlining the life and ministry of the hymn writer, interspersed with hymns by the writer. In other words, the message and music of the day is about and by the hymn writer (sort of like a musical biography).

Sermon Illustrations

Illustrating your sermon from the 2000 years of experiences in the church's history is one way of weaving a bit of history into what was not necessarily a moment for teaching church history.

Sermon Commentary

Rather than just use modern commentators when you seek to explain a text, why not mention how Christians in other centuries understood the passage? The IVP "Ancient Christian Commentary on Scripture" series is great for this perspective. You could also say something like "Christians in the eleventh century understood this passage to mean" or "The reformers such as Martin Luther or John Calvin taught that this text meant." Of course, referring to the past does not mean that the ancient interpretation is always right, it simply reminds your congregants of their place in a long tradition of those seeking to keep the faith.

Church History Quotes

Many people love a good quote, and the church's history is filled with them. The use of such quotes in your messages is one way of showing the richness and wisdom of the past.

Church Library

Invest in some good books and videos for your church library. Don't forget to get some kids material too! Try to avoid buying just historical novels, they are helpful but are not the most reliable source for history.

Anniversary Service

This is a natural time for talking about the past; in fact, people expect it! Make sure you take advantage of this opportunity by digging into your church's history and have it on display. Oral accounts of important events can also be an important part of the sharing of your church's story.

Drama

This is a labor-intensive form of teaching, but when historical dramas are done right they are very powerful.

Display Cabinet

Why not get someone to build a display cabinet to show off some of your church's artifacts? I remember finding a bunch of old trophies in a church that should have been on display. Instead, they were getting ruined in a box in a basement. Every church has important documents, pictures, old hymnals, publications, communion cups, plates, etc. that would be great additions to a display cabinet.

Art Work

I remember visiting a church in England that William Carey had once pastored. One whole wall had a mural painted that depicted his life and ministry in England and India. It was a powerful teaching tool, but also an inspirational account of one man's life in service to God. Churches should invest more in art that illustrates the past—art such as murals, stained glass windows, statues, pictures, etc.

Halloween, or Hallowed Eve

Some Christians do not like the violent and pagan elements in modern Halloween. One way to "Christianize" the day is to have your kids wander the streets dressed up as figures from church history, and/or have an event where everyone must come as a figure from church history. Dressing up as a figure from the church's history actually makes a lot of sense since November 1st is All Saints Day, the day in the church's calendar that celebrates the lives of our Christian forbearers.

Reformation Sunday

In many Protestant churches there is a tradition of celebrating the Reformation on one Sunday a year. This is a natural time for launching into some history!

Preparing Your
Local Church's History

At some time in your ministry you, or your church, may want to write a history of your local congregation. The following are some brief things to consider when going about compiling and writing such a history.

STAGE ONE: PRELIMINARY WORK

- Ask why you are doing it. Do not use the book to make a point, condemn a person or save your job.

- Will it be a chronicle or a history? Chronicles tend to be "just the facts," while a history will interpret. A chronicle tends to be "safer" and less controversial than a history.

- Don't recreate the wheel. See if you already have a written history. If you do, why not simply update the history (some are years old and could benefit from someone filling in the history up to the present day.)

- Some churches are fortunate enough to have an unofficial historian already present. You would be wise to work with such a person.

- Is someone going to be paid to write it? If so, who has final editorial power? Related to this is the question of whether or not it will be an "official" history. If so, the church leaders usually will want a final say as to the content.
- What sources are available? Will you be relying on oral sources? What is at your denominational archives?
- Who will publish it? Who will pay for publishing? Will it be print-on-demand (a growing preference for small circulation books)?

STAGE TWO: RESEARCHING THE HISTORY

- Make sure you get a timeline of key dates and leaders – this provides a framework and helps people place themselves in the larger history of the church.
- Look out for minefields! What are the issues that you need to be VERY careful about addressing (e.g. church splits, firings of leaders, broken relationships, etc.).
- Make sure you try to get a variety of voices on the controversial issues (e.g. splits, firings, etc.). You may want to stay away from these events as much as possible, or at least try to present a fair portrayal of the events (which may mean you provide the different perspectives on the events in question).
- Make good notes, and be able to find your sources if someone asks "why did you say that?" or "where did you get that idea?"
- Clarify confidentiality issues with written and oral sources.
- Including pictures in a book is always appreciated by readers (especially if they find themselves in the book!). If you cannot identify someone, leave the picture(s) in the foyer with a sheet of paper beside it asking for people to identify anything they can (e.g. people, event, location, etc.).

STAGE THREE: WRITING THE HISTORY

- Do you want multiple authors, or just one?
- Try to tell as story, not just dump facts on people.
- Make it as positive as possible (without skewing the facts).
- Relate the history to the events of the day (e.g. wartime, Depression, changing role of women in society, etc.).
- Make a few electronic copies of the text, and store in a variety of locations.

STAGE FOUR: CELEBRATING THE HISTORY

- Put a copy of the book in your denominational archives and in your local library.
- Send a copy to your denominational head office.
- Place a few in your church library.
- Make them available for members to purchase.
- Preserve the records that you found (e.g. place in the archives or in a safe place in the church building).
- Have a book-launching party at the church, and tie it into your anniversary service.
- Require members to read the book as preparation for membership.

CPSIA information can be obtained at www.ICGtesting.com
Printed in the USA
239630LV00003B/157/P